the POWER of SOCIAL MEDIA

Stuart A. Kallen

ReferencePoint
Press

San Diego, CA

About the Author

Stuart A. Kallen is the author of more than 350 nonfiction books for children and young adults. He has written on topics ranging from the theory of relativity to the art of electronic dance music. In 2018 Kallen won a Green Earth Book Award from the Nature Generation environmental organization for his book *Trashing the Planet: Examining the Global Garbage Glut*. In his spare time he is a singer, songwriter, and guitarist in San Diego.

Picture Credits:
Cover: Sfio Cracho/Shutterstock.com
    Tetiana Chernykova/Shutterstock.com
    Wayhome Studio/Shutterstock.com

 7: Twin Design/Shutterstock.com
11: AAraujo/Shutterstock.com
14: Antonello Marangi/Shutterstock.com
17: Rich Carey/Shutterstock.com
20: Tinseltown/Shutterstock.com
23: CRX PHOTO/Shutterstock.com

25: A. Mertens/Shutterstock.com
31: AlessandroBiascioli/Shuttestock.com
34: fyv6561/Shutterstock.com
36: Lyonstock/Shutterstock.com
41: Reuters/Alamy Stock Photo
43: Amit.pansuriva/Shutterstock.com
46: RaviNepz/Shutterstock.com
50: Ink Drop/Shutterstock.com
52: anut21ng Stock/Shutterstock.com
53: Ron Adar/Shutterstock.com

LIBRARY OF CONGRESS CATALOGING-IN-PUBLICATION DATA

Names: Kallen, Stuart A., 1955- author.
Title: The power of social media / by Stuart A. Kallen.
Description: San Diego, CA : ReferencePoint Press, 2022. | Includes bibliographical references and index.
Identifiers: LCCN 2021059565 (print) | LCCN 2021059566 (ebook) | ISBN 9781678203481 (library binding) | ISBN 9781678203498 (ebook)
Subjects: LCSH: Social media--Juvenile literature. | Social media--Psychological aspects--Juvenile literature. | Social control--Juvenile literature.
Classification: LCC HM742 .K3785 2022 (print) | LCC HM742 (ebook) | DDC 302.23/1--dc23/eng/20220204
LC record available at https://lccn.loc.gov/2021059565
LC ebook record available at https://lccn.loc.gov/2021059566

CONTENTS

INTRODUCTION

Motivating the Masses

In 2011, hundreds of thousands of protesters turned out in the streets of Cairo, Egypt, to protest against their corrupt president, Hosni Mubarak. Within weeks Mubarak, who had been running the country for thirty years, was driven from office. The uprising was one of the first in which protesters took to Twitter, YouTube, and Facebook to organize a successful mass demonstration. Users of social media helped spread the protests to neighboring countries, including Tunisia and Libya. Entrenched dictators were driven from office in what was called the Arab Spring. In the American press, social media was hailed as liberation technology, a new form of protest that gave average citizens leverage over the rich and powerful. University of Washington communications professor Phillip Howard supported this view in 2011 after analyzing more than 3 million Arab Spring tweets and thousands of YouTube videos and blog posts. "Social media," he said, "carried a cascade of messages about freedom and democracy across North Africa and the Middle East, and helped raise expectations for the success of political uprising."[1]

Ten years later, social media platforms were used in another government demonstration. In 2021 a group of violent demonstrators stormed the US Capitol in Washington, DC. Like the Egyptians, the Americans used Twitter, Facebook, and other sites to coordinate their actions. But this group was not trying to spread democracy; it was attempting to halt the democratic process that would make Joe Biden president after he won a free and fair election. The protesters based their actions on unsubstantiated claims about voter fraud and a stolen election that had been spreading on social media for months. Early tech investor and social media critic Roger McNamee expressed the views of many when he said, "Facebook and Google and Twitter . . . radicalized the people, and then gave them a platform for organizing this attack."[2]

A Mostly Negative Effect

The Arab Spring and the Capitol attack, separated by a decade, demonstrate the power of social media to prompt masses of people to act. The events also shows how the use of social media has changed since the popularity of Facebook and Twitter exploded during the first decade of the 2000s. Many observers and users stopped thinking of social media as liberation technology. Instead, the voices of critics now dominate, faulting social media platforms for provoking polarization and dispersing disinformation (lies that are deliberately spread to manipulate the public). According to a 2020 Pew Research Center poll, two-thirds of Americans said social media had a mostly negative effect on the direction of the country. Respondents blamed the technology for the spread of online bullying, conspiracy theories, hate speech, and political extremism. Only 10 percent said social media had a mostly positive effect, bringing people together, helping them share important issues, and promoting activism.

Many users arrive at their own negative opinion of social media simply from interacting with it every day. But these insights

were confirmed by former Facebook product manager Frances
Haugen in 2021. Haugen released
tens of thousands of pages of internal company documents that
revealed that Facebook's chief executive officer (CEO), Mark Zuckerberg, knows the platform is used
to propagate hatred and lies. But
this negative content is allowed to
circulate because it increases user engagement. Company research shows that angry, negative comments attract more likes
and shares than posts that are positive. Professor of social media
Andrew Selepak explains: "[Facebook] feeds us negative content
to get us to react negatively. Facebook has realized that to a large
extent, we want this experience. We sort of crave this experience
and we keep coming back to it for that same type of content. To
be riled up."[3]

Compiling User Data

Riled up people spend more time on Facebook. This leads them
to write more comments, click on additional content, and view
more ads. All this interaction allows Facebook to compile troves
of data about each user's age, hobbies, political interests, religious beliefs, spending habits, exercise regimens, sexual identity,
and even drug use. The company also casts a wide net for outside data, collecting information from apps that are used to manage health, exercise regimens, finances, entertainment choices,
and more.

Facebook gleans information by using artificial intelligence
(AI) to analyze the smallest personal details. The company tallies
the number of exclamation points and capital letters in a user's
comments and analyzes personal photos for various expressions.
Facebook even uses AI to monitor heart rate data from its Instant

Heart Rate app. All this information allows the company to make fine-grained predictions about what kinds of ads users will click on and what types of products they will buy. History professor Heather Cox Richardson argues, "[Facebook] profits from packaging users to sell to advertisers. Facebook has sliced and diced its users so that it can sell us with pinpoint accuracy."[4]

Although other social media companies receive their fair share of criticism, Facebook and Zuckerberg generate the most negative headlines for a reason. Facebook is by far the largest social media company in the world. With more than 3.5 billion active monthly users, Facebook is more than three times the size of TikTok and twelve times bigger than Twitter. And Zuckerberg holds a unique position in the tech industry. At other companies a CEO has to answer to a board of directors occupied by individuals who work together to shape company policies. Zuckerberg, however, owns 58 percent of Facebook stock, which gives him total

There are many popular social media platforms, each allowing users to connect in a slightly different way. These apps have brought about huge changes in the way people live, love, work, and play.

control over all decisions. As Haugen testified before Congress, "There are no similarly powerful companies that are as [individually] controlled. . . . There is no one currently holding Mark accountable but himself."[5] Haugen says this makes Zuckerberg the most powerful person on Earth.

The Good with the Bad

Facebook may be unique, but all social media platforms, including Twitter, YouTube, Snapchat, and TikTok, generate profits that same way. Although these companies attract criticism for the way they operate, they also contribute to the economy. Facebook says its apps, which include Instagram and WhatsApp, have created more than 3 million jobs in the social media marketing industry. They generated more than $228 billion in 2019. And almost everyone can agree that social media has brought about huge changes in the way people live, work, and play. Artists, musicians, professional gamers, and businesses large and small use social media to attract attention and make money in ways never before possible.

Around half of all people on Earth use some form of social media. Some might say they hate it, but social media is part of the fabric of life for billions of people. The average user spends 144 minutes a day social networking, an increase of 60 minutes a day over 2012, according to the data analytics company Statista. Although it sometimes seems the bad outweighs the good, social media has taken a center role in the modern world. And it will remain there as long as people use cellphones and computers.

Raising Awareness

In May 2020 George Floyd, an unarmed Black man, died after a Minneapolis police officer kneeled on his neck for nearly nine minutes during an arrest. A viral video of Floyd's death, taken by a bystander, touched off the largest protest movement in American history. Wherever people gathered, they held signs with the phrase *Black Lives Matter*. Although the phrase speaks for itself, its origins can be traced to social media. The Black Lives Matter (BLM) hashtag motivated social justice protesters who saw it on Twitter and Facebook. Millions rallied under the BLM banner to protest police killings in Kentucky, Colorado, Georgia, California, New York, and other states. And the movement quickly spread to nations throughout the world; BLM signs could be seen in the hands of protesters in Asia, South America, Africa, and the Middle East.

Black Lives Matter might be one of the best examples of social media being used to organize protests and inspire positive change. The movement began as a simple hashtag after the killing of a young Black man in Sanford, Florida. In 2011, seventeen-year-old Trayvon Martin was shot and killed by

George Zimmerman, a neighborhood watch coordinator. Zimmerman was acquitted of murder in 2013. Community activist Alicia Garza learned of Zimmerman's acquittal while watching the news in a bar in Oakland, California. Garza said she felt like she had been punched in the gut, and later, woke up crying in the middle of the night. Garza channeled her pain into what she called a love note to Black people: "Black people. I love you. I love us. Our lives matter. Black Lives Matter."[6] Garza posted her love letter on Facebook, and it attracted immediate attention. In Southern California one of Garza's close friends, Patrisse Cullors, shared the message and included a hashtag: *#BlackLivesMatter*. In New York City another friend, immigration rights organizer Opal Tometi, called Garza and offered to create a social media platform called Black Lives Matter that would utilize the slogan to launch a new civil rights movement.

In 2014 the phrase *Black Lives Matter* rose to prominence when a White police officer in Ferguson, Missouri, shot a young Black man named Michael Brown. Images of Brown's body lying in the street for more than four hours in the summer heat quickly went viral on Twitter. BLM hashtags, including #HandsUpDontShoot and #NoJusticeNoPeace, drove protesters into the streets. One of the most popular slogans, *Black Lives Matter*, was seen on dozens of protest signs. Few people had seen or heard that expression at the time, but in a matter of weeks the phrase provided a unifying message wherever social justice protests were held.

From Facebook to the Streets

Although some changes were instituted after the Ferguson protests, Black people were still too often the victims of police shootings. And social media continued to play an important role in highlighting these tragedies. In July 2016 a police officer shot and killed a thirty-two-year-old Black man named Philando Castile in the St. Paul, Minnesota, suburb of Falcon Heights. Castile was accompanied by his girlfriend, Diamond Reynolds, who livestreamed the encounter on Facebook. The graphic video shows Castile slumped in the car, dying from chest wounds. Reynolds later explained why she livestreamed the event. "I did it so that the world knows that these police are not here to protect and serve us," she claimed. "They are here to assassinate us. They are here to kill us because we are black."[7]

The Facebook post triggered large local protests within hours. Black Lives Matter activists and others throughout the country took to social media to protest Castile's shooting. Within days, 112 demonstrations were held in eighty-eight American cities. In Oakland, over one thousand protesters shut down Interstate 880 for several hours. In Minneapolis, activists blocked Interstate 94.

The BLM movement celebrated its fifth anniversary in 2018. By that time the BLM hashtag had been used 30 million times on Twitter alone. And the ongoing protests created a new generation of activists who utilized social media to call attention to ongoing racial injustice and bring about change. After Floyd's killing, teenage organizers spearheaded protests across the United States and in countries throughout the world. Singer Alicia Keys credits the

On March 12, 2015, marchers take to the streets to protest the police killing of Tony Robinson, a young Black man. Their Black Lives Matter banner references the now-famous movement, then just two years old.

deft use of social media for BLM's success. "Imagine if Martin Luther King and Malcolm X had Instagram. It would have been a whole other power network,"[8] she notes.

This new power network seemed to have changed public opinion about BLM nearly overnight. In a 2016 Pew poll of US voters, 43 percent of Americans said they supported the movement, and 18 percent said they strongly supported it. After the 2020 Floyd protests, Pew reported that 67 percent of Americans said they supported BLM, and the number of those who strongly supported it more than doubled. Support for BLM trended downward to around 55 percent in 2021. But the BLM hashtag remains active and is used by organizers to get out the vote, direct activists to lobby politicians, and organize protests whenever necessary. And the phrase *Black Lives Matter* has become embedded in American culture, appearing on bumper stickers, T-shirts, and yards signs years after the Floyd protests.

Changing the Conversation on Climate

In 2020 Swedish environmental activist Greta Thunberg said the BLM protests and the climate action movement were both driven by the same forces: "There are signs of change, of awakening. . . . The world has passed a social tipping point where it becomes impossible to look away. We cannot keep sweeping these things under the carpet, these injustices. People are starting to find their voice, to sort of understand that they can actually have an impact."[9]

Thunberg found her voice through the use of social media in 2018, when she was a fifteen-year-old student. She had little interest in the environmental movement until she discovered a climate justice group called Zero Hour on Instagram. The group is dedicated to slowing climate change while focusing on environmental justice for poor people who experience the greatest harm as the planet warms. Zero Hour was cofounded in Seattle in 2017 by a sixteen-year-old Colombian-born student named Jamie Margolin.

Like most successful activists, Margolin was a tech savvy organizer who used social media to recruit supporters, organize rallies, and lobby politicians. Thunberg participated in a Zero Hour demonstration in Stockholm in 2018. This was part of a worldwide protest that was organized through social media in about twenty-five other cities, including London; Washington, DC; and Nairobi, Kenya. After the protests, Thunberg and Margolin became friends through

The Trayvon Generation

Social media clearly changed the dynamics of the 2020 Black Lives Matter (BLM) protests. Some of the young activists leading the BLM marches are referred to as "the Trayvon generation"; they came of age between the shooting death of Black teenager Trayvon Martin by a vigilante in 2012 and the murder of George Floyd by a police officer in 2020. These activists learned about systemic racism and organized protests through Twitter, Facebook, and other sites.

In the wake of Floyd's death, six Nashville high school students, who met in a group text chat on Twitter, started a group called Teens 4 Equality. The students, who did not previously know one another, used free graphics, petitions, and educational materials available on the BLM website to spread their message of racial justice. They made a flyer and shared it on social media; ten thousand people showed up to their protest rally. One of the organizers, Emma Rose Smith, described how anyone can organize a demonstration: "If you want to make a protest, you can make a protest. . . . We are a lot more aware than our ancestors because of social media and I don't think we're going to make the same mistakes."

Quoted in Katie Kindelan, "6 Teen Girls Were the Organizers Behind Nashville's Massive Black Lives Matter Protests," *Good Morning America*, June 9, 2020. www.goodmorningamerica.com.

Instagram. Thunberg later recalled, "Before that I basically hadn't met any young person who seemed to care about the climate, the environment, or our future survival on the planet. . . . I remember feeling so alone, it seemed as if no one my age . . . wanted to make a difference—apart from people like Jamie Margolin."[10]

After taking part in the Zero Hour demonstration, Thunberg initiated a one-person environmental protest. She skipped out of her ninth-grade classes to sit outside the Swedish parliament holding a homemade sign that read "School Strike for Climate."[11] A reporter asked Thunberg what she was doing. She replied that she was planning to cut school every Friday until Sweden passed laws that drastically reduced carbon emissions. Two weeks later, Thunberg spoke at a climate rally in Stockholm, where she described climate change as a nightmare scenario in which little is being done to halt it.

Thunberg's dire message would soon inspire people throughout the world to hold climate strikes. After the story of her one-person protest was described in a local paper, her social media

Teenage environmental activist Greta Thunberg speaks at a climate change rally in Turin, Italy, on December 13, 2019. A flag supporting Thunberg's pet project, Fridays for Future, flies in the background.

account blew up. Thunberg's school strike movement, which she called Fridays for Future, went viral. Thunberg became an international sensation as her message on climate change galvanized activists all over the world.

Fridays for Future is a decentralized movement based on school strikes. Thousands of individual student activists use social media to organize climate strikes at their own schools. On March 15, 2019, during the first global School Climate Strike, over 1 million people demonstrated in 125 countries. In Albany, New York, senior Audrea Din recalled learning about the upcoming strike on Twitter. She set up a GoFundMe account that raised $1,000 in just a few days. Din used the money to set up a climate protest attended by two hundred students.

High school sophomore Kallan Benson helped bring together isolated supporters for the School Climate Strike in Washington, DC, using emails, text messages, and Slack to organize kids in Florida, Maryland, and elsewhere. Benson remarked, "We rely on social media to promote our strikes and get into the public psyche."[12]

By September 2019 social media activists had helped transform the climate strike movement into a massive worldwide phenomenon. An estimated 6 million people of all ages and backgrounds joined in international climate strikes known as the Global Week for Future. In what has been called the biggest climate protest ever held, people took to the streets in more than six hundred cities in the United States, Europe, Africa, and the Middle East.

From Hashtags to Activism

Few doubt that the power of social media can be harnessed to rapidly publicize and organize demonstrations. But movements that form practically overnight can fade from the public view just as quickly. People who do little more than sign online petitions, retweet memes, and add supportive comments to trending so-

Hashtag–Flooding Activists

Social media activism has elevated the hashtag to a position of unprecedented power. Some who want to counter online negativity have used a technique called hashtag flooding to drown out hate speech and racism. Hashtag flooding involves hijacking a hashtag to change the conversation. And in 2020 one of the most successful hashtag-flooding campaigns came from an unexpected source: ardent K-pop fans.

Social media helped spread K-pop music and culture throughout the world, and K-pop fans are highly organized online; K-pop Twitter accounted for more than 6 billion tweets in 2019. The fans took on racists and radical right-wing groups during the George Floyd protests. At the time, hashtags associated with racist groups such as QAnon and the Proud Boys were used to spread violent speech and disinformation about BLM. Millions of K-pop fans drowned out the hate by using the hashtags to post K-pop TikToks, gay-rights memes, fan photos, and other harmless material. Activist Igor Volsky explains that "the power of taking over hashtags . . . [demonstrates] that those kinds of hateful messages don't represent us and don't represent what we believe. And we're going to use our power—the power of numbers—to flood and overtake those hateful messages with messages of love and hope."

Quoted in Nicole Gallucci, "2020 Was the Year Activists Mastered Hashtag Flooding," Mashable, December 30, 2020. https://mashable.com.

cial justice posts are practicing what is called hashtag activism. In the past, major social problems were solved by activists working long hours to convince a majority of citizens—and their elected representatives—to support changing laws. Hashtag activists cannot always be counted on to stick with a movement through drawn-out processes such as raising money, lobbying politicians, passing legislation, and instituting social change. And social media activism has other limitations as well, according to sixteen-year-old Dutch climate activist Erik Christiansson. "On social media, often your posts get seen by other people who already agree with you and you don't really get that much attention from outside,"[13] he says.

Although Christiansson makes a good point, hashtag activism can be hard to ignore at times. In 2020 activists hijacked hashtags associated with racist right-wing groups and drowned out their posts with social justice posts. This type of activity proves that Twitter, Facebook, and other social media platforms are still the fastest, cheapest, and most efficient way to get a message out to a massive audience. This was confirmed by a 2021 poll conducted by the Pew Research Center. Pollsters found that millennials (people born between 1980 and 1996) and Gen Zers (those born after 1996 and part of Generation Z) exhibit high levels of engagement on issues surrounding climate change. Around 30 percent of this demographic has taken action, such as donating money or contacting elected officials. This compares to around 20 percent of older Americans in the Gen X and baby boom generations. As Pew researchers Alec Tyson, Brian Kennedy, and Cary Funk write, this activism is spurred by social media. They say, "Compared with

> "On social media, often your posts get seen by other people who already agree with you and you don't really get that much attention from outside."[13]
>
> —Erik Christiansson, climate activist

Rainforest jungle in Borneo, Malaysia, is destroyed to make way for oil palm plantations. Activists share photos like this on social media to spread awareness of environmental issues as they happen.

older adults, Gen Zers and Millennials are talking more about the need for action on climate change; among social media users, they are seeing more climate change content online; and they are doing more to get involved with the issue through activities such as volunteering and attending rallies and protests."[14]

The younger generation, united through social media, is getting harder to ignore. This was clear during the 2021 United Nations Climate Change Conference of the Parties (COP26) in Glasgow, Scotland. When Thunberg arrived at COP26, she was treated like a rock star by reporters, climate campaigners, delegates, and politicians. Although Thunberg never intended to become an environmental brand or a climate influencer, social media made her one of the most recognized activists in the world. When she makes a statement, her words zoom around the world on countless digital devices, stirring others to join the climate movement and work locally to improve conditions globally. This inspiration is sometimes called "the Greta effect" in the media. The Greta effect inspired young climate activist Vanessa Nakate, who is raising awareness about climate change in Uganda, and Nicki Becker, who teaches other students about global warming in Argentina. Though separated by thousands of miles, these young activists connect through social media posts that spread messages with photos and videos of drought-stricken farms, flooded cities, clear-cut forests, and endangered animals.

Young people are the loudest voices challenging world leaders to act immediately on climate disaster, civil rights, and other issues. Enabled by phones, tablets, laptops, and other digital devices, their minute-by-minute messages show the power of social media to raise awareness and institute change.

The Influence of Influencers

Charli D'Amelio describes herself as "a normal teenager that a lot of people like to watch, for some reason."[15] D'Amelio might be normal, but she is also modest. What she describes as "a lot of people" translated to more than 128 million TikTok followers who gave her 10 billion likes in 2021. This made D'Amelio the most-followed TikTok personality of the year and one of the hottest social media stars in the world.

In 2019, at age fifteen, D'Amelio rose to fame when she began posting dance videos to trending songs on TikTok. Although millions of teenagers post similar videos to the site, D'Amelio had an advantage. She began dancing when she was three, and when she uploaded her debut video, she had been a competitive dancer for ten years. TikTokers responded to her videos immediately, and her fame increased every day. Within a few months, D'Amelio was performing live alongside pop singer Bebe Rexha. Her TikTok fame also landed her a spot in a Super Bowl commercial and a Disney television special. In 2021 D'Amelio was still coming to terms with her skyrocketing fame. "It doesn't make sense in my head," she says, "but I'm working on understanding it."[16]

Social Media Marketing

D'Amelio is one of thousands of dancers, singers, entertainers, comedians, gamers, and personalities who would be normal teenagers if not for social media. These TikTokers, YouTubers, and Instafamous influencers make millions of dollars from their billions of hits. They are paid by advertisers who understand the clout social media stars exert over young consumers, who spend an average of more than four hours a day on their mobile devices. This trend drives a powerful social media marketing industry that views major celebrities as *superinfluencers*, those with around fifty thousand followers as *microinfluencers*, and preteen toy reviewers such as Ryan Kaji as *kidfluencers*.

It is easy to understand why Kaji is able to earn millions of dollars a year. According to a 2019 Morning Consult poll, around one-third of Gen Zers say they trust influencers on YouTube more than they do police, politicians, and news anchors. And 44 percent of Gen Z consumers say they made purchasing decisions based on the recommendation of an influencer. This has created a social media gold rush as nearly every

TikTok superstar Charli D'Amelio attends the 10th Annual LACMA ART+FILM GALA in Los Angeles, California, on November 6, 2021. In 2021 she had more than 128 million TikTok followers. This made her the most-followed TikTok personality of the year.

Instagram and Molly Russell

To her parents, Molly Russell seemed like a normal fourteen-year-old London schoolgirl. But Russell was spending most of her free time scrolling through Instagram, which was filled with "bleak, depressive material, graphic self-harm content, and suicide encouraging memes," according to a report by the Royal College of Psychiatrists. In November 2017, while the rest of her family watched television and laughed together, Russell logged onto Instagram one last time. Then she took her own life. Her father, Ian Russell, later stated, "I have no doubt that social media helped kill my daughter."

According to the US Centers for Disease Control and Prevention, suicide is the second-leading cause of death for young people ages fifteen to twenty-four, surpassed only by accidents. Numerous complex factors drive individuals to take their own lives, including exposure to violence, social isolation, and clinical depression. Although these problems cannot be blamed on social media, those who are vulnerable are more likely to be affected by the negativity that can be found on the darker corners of the internet.

After the death of his daughter, Ian Russell set up a suicide prevention organization called the Molly Rose Foundation. The foundation's website offers online and in-person help to anyone who needs it.

Quoted in Tess de la Mare and Milo Boyd, "Girl Saw Social Media Posts 'Too Disturbing for Police' Before Taking Her Life," *The Mirror*, September 26, 2020. www.mirror.co.uk.

major brand has significantly increased its influencer marketing budget since 2019.

Major corporations work with influencer marketing directors at advertising agencies to hire Instagram stars, bloggers, YouTubers, and TikTokers who can create social media buzz around their clients' products. Marketers are most interested in social media influencers who have already built their own brand online and have a large audience that follows their videos, photos, blogs, and other posts.

Depending on the platform, influencers are paid to display ads that play before a video starts. They earn money from banner and sidebar ads that are visible at all times. Influencers are also paid to personally promote makeup, clothes, electronics, and other consumer goods. They use this power to sway the purchasing decisions of their fans and followers. These promotions build what marketers call digital chatter—that is, people talking about their products online. Google, which owns YouTube, pays influencers through its AdSense program, which keeps a tally on every user click on every video. Although figures vary, AdSense generally pays an average of $3 to $5 for every thousand views. Google keeps 45 percent, so a YouTuber earns a little less than ten dollars for every thousand views.

Getting paid millions to post videos sounds like an amazing job. Not surprisingly, 86 percent of young Americans say they want to become social media influencers, according to Morning Consult. However, anyone planning a career as a YouTuber, TikToker, or other social media influencer needs to conduct a reality check. In 2018 German science professor Mathias Bärtl analyzed YouTube statistics and discovered that the top 3 percent of creators earned the bulk of YouTube's advertising payouts. According to Bärtl, the other 97 percent of wannabe YouTubers who participated in AdSense earned less than $12,140 annually. This is considered a poverty wage for a single person in the United States.

The economics of social media are even worse on TikTok. This is something Jake Sweet, known as Surfaceldn on TikTok, understands only too well. Sweet makes fun, craft-based videos that attracted over 3 million followers in 2020. His TikTok influence gained him an invite to the 2021 MTV Video Music Awards, where he partied with the rich and famous. But Sweet says the site only pays him enough to buy groceries every month. And he spends most of the money purchasing materials for his next video.

Fakes and Frauds

Sweet knows it is hard to make an honest living on social media. But it is easier for those who are willing to engage in what is called influencer fraud. Social media fraudsters pump up their numbers by paying operations called click farms to provide phony followers. Click farms are mostly based in developing nations such as India, China, and the Philippines. Most click farm operations em-

Click farms in developing nations employ low-wage workers to like, share, comment on, subscribe to, and review social media posts. This interaction boosts the posts' popularity and visibility.

ploy large groups of low-wage workers to like, share, comment, subscribe, and review social media posts. This fake engagement manipulates algorithms on social media platforms to create more engagement with a paying client's posts.

A 2021 study by the social media analytics company HypeAuditor showed that more than half of all Instagram influencers (55 percent) engaged in some sort of social media fraud. Perhaps it is no surprise that the worst fakers were those with more than a million followers. Around two-thirds of the biggest Instagram celebrities and influencers have used click farms to buy followers, story reviews, and engagement with comment pods (where influencers get together and engage with one another's posts). Creating the illusion of popularity on social media is not expensive. Users can buy up to one thousand followers on Instagram for sixteen dollars or splurge on YouTube by spending fifty dollars. But influencer fraud is expensive for advertisers, who spent an estimated $1.6 billion on fraudsters in 2020, according to a study by the University of Baltimore.

Promoting Unhealthy Products

Some advertisers might be hurt when they pay for influencers with little real-world influence. But fakery in a different form can harm those who use social media—and many of them are young and female. A Morning Consult poll from 2021 reveals that one-third of Gen Z women follow many influencers, and half of those polled say they follow at least a few. Most of the women in the survey said they tend to favor Instagram, where beauty and fashion are the most popular topics.

In 2021 Kylie Jenner was one of the most popular influencers on Instagram, with more than 278 million followers. Jenner was only nine years old when she made her television debut as the youngest sister on the show *Keeping Up With the Kardashians*. The show, which premiered in 2007, followed the lives of sisters Kourtney, Kim, and Khloé Kardashian and their half sisters, Kylie and Kendall Jenner. *Keeping Up With the Kardashians* was an instant hit, making household names out of Jenner and the rest of her family. The show ended its long run in 2021.

> "It's the power of social media. I had such a strong reach before I was able to start [any business]."[17]
>
> —Kylie Jenner, social media influencer

Over the years, Jenner grew from a shy kid into an attractive young woman with a great fashion sense. By the time she was sixteen, Jenner was earning millions from clothing promotional deals and her own line of cosmetics. In 2019, at the age of twenty-one, Jenner became the first self-made Gen Z billionaire. As one of the most followed people on Instagram, Jenner can charge advertisers more than $1.2 million for a single post promoting a product. As Jenner explains, "It's the power of social media. I had such a strong reach before I was able to start anything."[17]

Like many fashionista influencers, Jenner has been accused by critics of promoting impossible beauty standards to susceptible young women. She is one of many influencers, including her

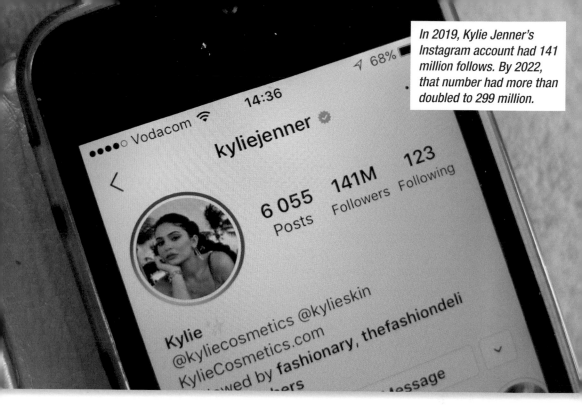

sister Kim Kardashian and rapper Cardi B, who endorse diet and detox teas that contain an herb known as senna, an extremely powerful laxative. Senna is used by doctors to treat constipation and to clear the intestines before colonoscopy diagnostic tests. Senna causes temporary water weight loss by sending users to the bathroom more often. Although Jenner might look beautiful and perfectly composed when posing with a package of diet tea on Instagram, those who ingest senna experience stomach cramps, diarrhea, and the inability to control their bowel movements. Drinking diet teas on a regular basis is extremely unhealthy. They prevent the body from properly absorbing nutrients and calories from food. And senna can cause the intestines to become dependent on it. Once stopped, this can lead to constipation, bloating, and, ironically, weight gain.

Harming Mental Health

Instagram came under fire in 2021 when leaked Facebook research revealed the app worsened body image issues for one in three teen girls. The report, which surveyed more than twenty-five hundred teens in the United States and the United Kingdom, revealed that Instagram made young women feel unattractive and negative about their bodies. One female British respondent to the survey said, "You can't ever win on social media. If you're curvy, you're too busty. If you're skinny, you're too skinny. If you're bigger, you're too fat. But it's clear you need . . . to be thin, to be pretty. It's endless, and you just end up feeling worthless."[18]

Around 10 percent of users surveyed said they wanted to kill themselves because of Instagram. But according to the report, Instagram users "often feel 'addicted' [to the app] and know that what they're seeing is bad for their mental health but feel unable to stop themselves."[19]

> "We cannot be sure if . . . Instagram caused teenagers to become depressed [or if] . . . depressed teenagers are more likely than others to use Instagram."[20]
>
> —Laurence Steinberg, professor of psychology

Although the Facebook survey was revealing, it was not a rigorous scientific study that could prove Instagram is harmful to users. Additionally, even those who said Instagram made them feel bad about their bodies also said they thought the app was useful and enjoyable at times. Noting the mixed results of the study, psychology professor Laurence Steinberg explains, "We cannot be sure if . . . Instagram caused teenagers to become depressed [or if] . . . depressed teenagers are more likely than others to use Instagram, or to use it more often."[20]

TikTok Too

Much of the criticism over social media in 2021 was aimed at Instagram. But studies show that harmful dieting and eating disorder hashtags are also in abundance on TikTok, one of the most popular sites in the world among users between the ages of sixteen and twenty-four. According to Bridget Todd, spokesperson for

The Science of Addiction

Internal research at Facebook, leaked to the press in 2021, revealed that the company's Instagram platform left young users feeling addicted to the app. Derek Thompson, a staff writer for *The Atlantic*, compares Instagram to alcohol: "Delightful but also depressing, a popular experience that blends short-term euphoria with long-term regret, a product that leads to painful and even addictive behavior among a significant minority."

This addictive behavior is linked to the way human brains are wired. When people engage in enjoyable activities, their brains release a pleasure-inducing chemical called dopamine. This chemical is also produced by some drugs. Social media use also releases dopamine in the brains of people whose feeds are racking up likes and followers. This causes users to feel excited and happy when new notifications pop up. However, the more dopamine users get, the more they want. This anticipation causes people to continually check their phones for notifications. When notifications do not appear, users craving a dose of dopamine can feel anxious and depressed. Rather than put down the phone, they post again and again, hoping their numbers will increase. This can lead to a social media addiction that can be very hard to break.

Derek Thompson, "Social Media Is Attention Alcohol," *The Atlantic*, September 17, 2021. www.theatlantic.com.

the women's advocacy group UltraViolet, "TikTok as a platform is flying under the radar right now. Everybody knows that Facebook and Instagram have a huge potential for harm when it comes to younger audiences, but we are not talking enough about the dangers of these newer platforms."[21]

Todd blames TikTok's "For You" page, where AI algorithms recommend videos based on a user's history. Analysts who searched for diet-related content were quickly led to videos promoting unhealthy fasting regimens, unproven appetite suppressants, and extreme weight-loss programs. The Chinese company that owns TikTok, ByteDance, does not allow content that encourages eating disorders, but users have found ways to elude human content monitors and AI programs.

Critics say videos are only part of the problem with TikTok. The site's augmented reality camera filters also promote a negative body message. There are dozens of filters on the site that allow users to change the appearance of their skin, face, and body shape. Todd says this creates an "impossible standard of beauty"[22] among young girls.

In America, TikTok works with the National Eating Disorders Association to provide educational resources from medical institutions and nutritional experts on the site. But thwarting the desires of teens bent on posting eating disorder content might be an impossible task. According to seventeen-year-old Jonna Nielsen, eating disorders on TikTok "spread like a disease. One person talks about it, then another person gets the idea to do the same thing. . . . It is ruining people's lives."[23]

Seek Serenity

In 2021 the global beauty industry generated $500 billion in annual sales, and the weight-loss market brought in about half that amount. Industry profits are driven by social media celebrities whose faces and bodies might be altered by a combination of augmented reality filters, extreme exercise, diet supplements. and plastic surgery. Social media platforms intermingle these fraudulently fabulous images with photos posted by users and their friends. This can leave average users feeling inadequate, anxious, and depressed as they compare themselves to influencers.

Experts say the best way to feel better while using social media is to disable notifications from social media apps, set limits for the amount of time spent on the platforms, and dedicate more time to hobbies, hiking, biking, sports, and other real-life activities. Some even pursue a total social media cleanse by turning off their phones and putting them away for a while. A 2019 study by researchers in Finland found that students who went for five days without social media experienced an increased "sense of serenity."[24] Although some still had fears of missing out, they felt empowered because they were in control of their lives—rather than being controlled by their phones.

Spreading Fear, Mistrust, and Lies

In 2019 Carol Smith joined Facebook and became one of the site's 1.9 billion daily users. Smith's profile described her as a conservative mother from Wilmington, North Carolina. Her interests included parenting, politics, and Christianity. Smith followed then-president Donald Trump and Fox News on Facebook. Her profile never indicated she was interested in conspiracy theories, yet within two days of joining, Smith's news feed began recommending groups associated with the QAnon movement.

QAnon began in 2017 when a mysterious internet user named "Q Clearance Patriot" began posting outrageous far-right and anti-Semitic conspiracy theories on an obscure message board. By 2019 QAnon had attracted millions of followers and had gained international attention. QAnon adherents believe, without evidence, that liberal celebrities and Democratic politicians belong to a secret cabal of Satan-worshipping pedophiles. Posts by Q falsely claim that this evil cabal runs an international child sex-trafficking ring and members drink the blood of children to stay young. According to QAnon message boards from 2018, President Trump was purportedly waging a secret war against these criminals and was poised to conduct mass arrests during a coming reckoning that supporters referred to as The Storm.

Despite showing no interest in QAnon, Smith's feed was soon flooded with posts from hundreds of groups linked to the movement. Many of the posts were filled with hate speech, racist and sexist comments, and misinformation that openly violated Facebook rules. Smith never clicked on any of the QAnon groups recommended by Facebook—because she is not a real person. Smith was an invented test user made up by a Facebook researcher. The employee was studying the role Facebook recommendations play in spreading falsehoods and divisiveness. The unnamed researcher wrote a report titled *Carol's Journey to QAnon*, which claims Smith's Facebook experience was marked by "a barrage of extreme, conspiratorial, and graphic content."[25]

Down the Rabbit Hole

Conspiracy theories are as old as humanity. But thanks to social media, there has never been a more efficient system for spreading misinformation across the world. Irrational ideas that used to exist on the fringes of society have been adopted by millions of people who have fallen into social media rabbit holes. The journey to the darkest conspiracy theories on the internet often begins with someone searching for wellness, religious, or political content. Within seconds, algorithms push fake news sites and extremist content to the top of the user's news feed. This is something Melissa Rein Lively has come to understand only too well.

In 2020 Lively owned a successful marketing company in Scottsdale, Arizona. But loneliness and boredom brought on by the COVID-19 pandemic lockdown pushed her to spend more time scrolling through her Facebook feed. Lively was al-

When the COVID-19 pandemic began, most people began wearing face masks to prevent the virus from spreading. Some people, however, believed lies spread on social media that face masks were a form of government control.

ready a member of a few New Age wellness groups. She soon found herself clicking on Facebook recommendations linked to QAnon groups with up to fifty thousand members. Lively came to believe lies about face masks people wore during the pandemic to slow the spread of COVID-19. In her social media comments, she called masks "muzzles" and came to believe they were a form of government control. In July 2020, Lively walked into a local Target store and destroyed a mask display while workers watched in dismay. She posted a self-made video of the incident, which went viral, drawing over 100 million views worldwide. When she was arrested, Lively told police she was a QAnon spokesperson. After a psychiatric interview, Lively was involuntarily committed to a mental health facility. She later described her experience: "I was all consumed with doom-scrolling on the Internet. I was living in these conspiracy theories. All of this fear porn that I was consuming online was just feeding my depression and anxiety."[26]

"I was living in these conspiracy theories. All of this fear porn that I was consuming online was just feeding my depression and anxiety."[26]

—Melissa Rein Lively, former conspiracy theorist

Lively suffered from a mental breakdown that nearly destroyed her marketing company and her marriage. After attending an eight-week trauma program at an Arizona rehabilitation facility, she came to see how she fell down the QAnon rabbit hole. And perhaps it is not surprising that Lively utilized the power of social media to redeem herself. She started a YouTube channel to discuss the link between mental health and conspiracy theories.

Algorithms in Charge

The rabbit hole problem is not confined to Facebook. Around 70 percent of the clicks made by users on YouTube are recommended by the site's algorithms. This sophisticated software powered by AI determines which videos will appear in a user's "Up Next" sidebar. YouTube employees have said this conveyer belt of videos is key for the company's growth. The recommended videos keep users glued to their screens, which exposes them to more ads. But independent research shows that the recommendations on YouTube—like those on Facebook—tend to steer users to violent, radical content. Tristan Harris is a former design ethicist at Google, YouTube's parent company. Describing why so many are pushed to conspiracy theory videos, he claims, "There's a spectrum on YouTube between the calm section . . . and Crazytown, where the extreme stuff is. If I'm YouTube and I want you to watch more, I'm always going to steer you toward Crazytown."[27]

> "There's a spectrum on YouTube between the calm section . . . and Crazytown, where the extreme stuff is. If I'm YouTube . . . I'm always going to steer you toward Crazytown."[27]
>
> —Tristan Harris, design ethicist

All major social media companies rely on algorithms to determine what users see and hear. And all companies say that their formulas are top secret; they do not want competitors copying their algorithms, nor do they want users to game the system in ways that push their posts to the top. But the public release of

Misinformation Gets More Clicks

There are two principal organizations that study the spread of misinformation by media organizations on Facebook. NewsGuard and Media Bias/Fact Check classify thousands of Facebook news publishers by their political viewpoints from far left to far right. Each news source is rated as accurate or untrustworthy. Data analysis of this information conducted by New York University (NYU) showed that untrustworthy pages filled with misinformation generated six times more user engagement than accurate news.

The NYU study looked at posts uploaded during the run-up and aftermath of the 2020 presidential election from August 2020 to January 2021. Although misinformation was found across the political spectrum, news sources on the right published much more misinformation than those on the left. Rebekah Tromble, director of the Institute for Data, Democracy & Politics at the George Washington University, reviewed the study's findings. Tromble said, "[The research] helps add to the growing body of evidence that, despite a variety of mitigation efforts, misinformation has found a comfortable home—and an engaged audience—on Facebook." But as Tromble notes, as long as misinformation generates the most clicks—and the most user engagement—there is little motivation for the company to remove it.

Quoted in Elizabeth Dwoskin, "Misinformation on Facebook Got Six Times More Clicks than Factual News During the 2020 Election, Study Says," *Washington Post*, September 4, 2021. www.washingtonpost.com.

Facebook's internal documents in 2021 reveals how the company determines what users see at the top of their news feed. Artificial intelligence algorithms analyze up to ten thousand data points that relate to the user's history and the number of reactions and comments a post receives. As users scroll down, they see posts in an order tailored to their viewing habits. But the most important determining factor in what users see is Facebook's desire to keep them scrolling for the longest period of time while viewing ads.

Facebook algorithms are set to give great weight to the so-called reaction emojis under each post and comment. In 2016 reaction emojis that represent love, humor, surprise, sadness, and anger were added alongside the iconic blue thumbs-up "like" button. Unbeknownst to its billions of users, Facebook researchers

Facebook's standard set of "reaction emojis" allow users to register seven responses to posts: like, love, caring, laughing, surprised, sad, and angry.

were intensely tracking the new emojis. They found that posts that attracted the most anger, surprise, or sadness were the ones that kept users scrolling for longer periods. In 2017 Facebook set its algorithms to treat posts accompanied by the new emojis as five times more important than those that received only likes. As a result of this change, controversial posts that inspired anger were 500 percent more likely to be pushed to the top of users' news feeds.

Although algorithms are simply mathematical formulas that provide a computer with a command, the way they are used is subject to intense deliberations at companies such as Facebook. Software engineers, research teams, and data scientists spend their workdays debating the good and bad created by algorithms. The angry emoji was especially controversial. Internal company documents reveal that posts that generated anger could "[open] the door to more spam/abuse/clickbait."[28] This analysis proved correct. Research in 2019 showed that the angry emoji was closely associated with posts that included misinformation and disinformation.

Before and After the Election

Misinformation and disinformation fueled one of the most disastrous political events in recent American history. On January 6, 2021, the US Congress was voting to certify the election of a new president, Joseph Biden. During the proceedings, an angry mob stormed the Capitol in Washington, DC, in an attempt to illegally overturn the election that Donald Trump had lost. At least 138 police officers were injured in the melee, one rioter was killed, and four other deaths were attributed to incidents that occurred that day. Rioters ransacked offices of congressional representa-

Small Number of Anti-Vaxxers Spread Falsehoods

When vaccines were introduced in early 2021 to prevent the spread of COVID-19, most people were overjoyed, believing that the end of the long pandemic was in sight. But almost immediately misleading and false claims about the vaccine began to proliferate on Facebook, Instagram, Twitter, and other social media sites. Vaccine opponents, called anti-vaxxers, liked and shared these posts millions of times. But a June 2021 report from the Center for Countering Digital Hate discovered that 65 percent of the online anti-vaccine disinformation could be traced to just twelve people. The center labeled these anti-vaxxers "the Disinformation Dozen." Members of this group state without evidence that COVID does not exist or that the vaccines have numerous harmful side effects. Some of those in the Disinformation Dozen sell expensive nutritional supplements they falsely claim can prevent or treat the disease.

After NPR published a story about the Disinformation Dozen, Facebook removed sixteen associated accounts and placed restrictions on twenty-two others. Twitter suspended two accounts. As with other fraudsters, anti-vaxxers quickly found ways to skirt the bans. And COVID continued to spread as millions of people throughout the world repeated the false claims about the vaccine perpetuated by the Disinformation Dozen.

Quoted in Shannon Bond, "Just 12 People Are Behind Most Vaccine Hoaxes on Social Media, Research Shows," NPR, May 14, 2021. www.npr.org.

tives and caused more than $30 million in damages to the Capitol chambers, according to building manager J. Brett Blanton. Once again, Facebook was at the center of controversy as its products, including Instagram and WhatsApp, were used by rioters to coordinate their activities—and brag about them on social media.

No one can blame any social media company for the events of January 6, but Facebook has been singled out because it took measures to prevent chaos before the election. However, these policies were halted after the election.

In early 2020, during the run-up to the election, Facebook formed what it called the Civic Integrity team to monitor political posts. The team worked to ban election-related misinformation, racist comments, and foreign interference. Company employees worked overtime to remove groups that posted violent political content and instituted special algorithms to automatically delete hate speech. After a peaceful conclusion to the election, Facebook employees breathed a sigh of relief. As one unnamed employee said, "It was like we could take a victory lap. . . . There was a lot of . . . high-fiving in the office."[29]

Facebook managers, feeling they had done a good job, disbanded the Civic Integrity team. However, the action might have been premature. In dozens of statements and tweets, Trump claimed—without any evidence—that the election was stolen and he was the rightful winner. Those claims gave rise to the Stop the Steal movement by Trump supporters, which experienced dramatic growth after November 3.

Facebook analysts watched with alarm as comments on the page belonging to the main Stop the Steal group filled with "angry vitriol and a slew of conspiracy theories,"[30] according to a company report. Within two days, Stop the Steal grew to over 360,000 members, with thousands joining every hour. Facebook took a fragmented approach with Stop the Steal as it continued

Trump supporters marched at a Stop the Steal rally on November 7, 2020. They were protesting the outcome of the 2020 presidential election, which they incorrectly believed was awarded to Joe Biden due to voter fraud and an incomplete vote count.

to grow. The group's main page was removed from the platform, but dozens of affiliated groups were left intact. According to Facebook's own reports, these copycat groups were filled with QAnon content, white supremacist expressions, and calls to violence.

Whistleblower Frances Haugen had worked on the Civic Integrity team. After the election, Haugen saw users outwitting the systems meant to stop the spread of misinformation by using words and terms that did not specifically break the rules. This allowed influential users, including Trump, to spread claims of a stolen election without violating the platform's terms of service.

Facebook representatives often point out that they are required to make hard choices when it comes to political activities. The company says it is dedicated to allowing users to freely express themselves, even if the language might be viewed by some as divisive or offensive. As a Facebook report leaked by Haugen explained, "We recently saw non-violating content delegitimizing the U.S. election results go viral on our platforms. The majority . . . could be [viewed] as reasonable doubts about election processes, and so we did not feel comfortable intervening on such content."[31] But critics pointed out that the inaction facilitated the January insurrection and cautioned that free speech has its limits when it is used to incite riots.

> "Facebook . . . will have to continue to grapple with the problem of what to do about political leaders who abuse social media to spread lies and incite violence."[32]
>
> —Paul M. Barrett, law professor

After January 6, Facebook took the extraordinary step of banning Trump indefinitely from its platform. New York University law professor Paul M. Barrett stated, "The practical effect of this decision will be that Facebook—and possibly other platforms . . . will have to continue to grapple with the problem of what to do about political leaders who abuse social media to spread lies and incite violence."[32]

Views, News, and Conspiracies

While social media companies grapple with issues such as free speech and disinformation, the damage continues to resonate throughout the country. A 2021 CNN poll found that around half of all Americans know somebody who believes in a conspiracy theory posted on Facebook. That number is higher among younger Americans; 61 percent of adults younger than thirty-five say they know someone who supports a conspiracy theory based on Facebook content. Perhaps this is not surprising since 45 percent of Americans say they get their news from Facebook.

Facebook defenders point out that the site adds half a million new users every day—six new profiles per second. This leaves the platform struggling to monitor those who use it to spread lies. And as Facebook CEO Zuckerberg pointed out in 2021 after Haugen testified before Congress, spreading disinformation is not a good business practice. "The argument that we deliberately push content that makes people angry for profit is deeply illogical," he said. "We make money from ads, and advertisers consistently tell us they don't want their ads next to harmful or angry content. And I don't know any tech company that sets out to build products that make people angry or depressed. The moral, business and product incentives all point in the opposite direction."[33]

> "I don't know any tech company that sets out to build products that make people angry or depressed."[33]
>
> —Mark Zuckerberg, Facebook CEO

Zuckerberg has a lot to defend. Facebook made a profit of more than $29 billion in 2020, according to company financial statements. During a tumultuous year marked by a pandemic and a divisive election, people relied on Facebook more than ever to stay in touch. And as long as people look to social media to find facts and news about current events, bad actors will upload as much misinformation as platforms allow. This leaves it up to individual users to decide whether they want to believe unsubstantiated claims posted on social media.

CHAPTER FOUR

Social Media or Social Control?

Peng Shuai made history in 2014. She was the first Chinese tennis player to be ranked number one by the Women's Tennis Association (WTA) in women's doubles competitions. Peng went on to become a three-time Olympian and a two-time Grand Slam tennis champion in doubles. By 2021 Peng, who was still competing on the tennis court, had more than 574,000 followers on Weibo, the Chinese equivalent of Twitter.

On November 2, 2021, Peng dropped a bombshell on Weibo that sent shockwaves through the tennis world. Peng wrote a long post explaining that she had been sexually assaulted in 2018 by a powerful Chinese politician, Vice Premier Zhang Gaoli. Peng's disclosure was taken down by Chinese officials within thirty minutes, and her name and allegations were quickly scrubbed from Chinese social media. Searches for the names *Peng* or *Zhang* came up blank. Even innocent keywords such as *tennis* were censored. But screenshots of the sixteen-hundred-word post were already flooding other social media sites, including Twitter. (Twitter is not available to most people in China, but some find ways to elude government censorship.)

As the controversy began making headlines around the world, Peng disappeared; she was not seen in public or heard from for several weeks. Those who played against Peng, including tennis superstar Serena Williams, expressed concern on social media by using the hashtag #WhereIsPengShuai.

Peng's disappearance occurred at a sensitive time for the Chinese government. The nation was scheduled to host the 2022 Winter Olympics, which would bring billions of dollars into the country and present China in its best light. As alarm about Peng's whereabouts spread, there were calls to boycott the games.

Around three weeks after Peng's disappearance, something unusual happened. China's state-run television network published a screenshot on Twitter that was purportedly an email written by Peng to WTA chairman Steve Simon. Peng said the sexual assault allegations were not true and added, "I'm not missing, nor am I unsafe. I've just been resting at home and everything is fine."[34] However, few believed this post was written or sent by Peng. The email had no dateline, subject, or user address, and the language was awkward. The email, written in English, could not be found on Chinese social media.

A Flood of Propaganda

China is ruled by the Chinese Communist Party (CCP), which has a long history of forcing dissidents to write retractions or apologies for making critical statements. Some have been jailed for exposing abusive public officials. Those who are aware of this phenomenon say the language of Peng's post sounded like a forced confession. Simon stated, "I have a hard time believing that Peng Shuai actually wrote the email we received or believes what is being attributed to her."[35]

> "I have a hard time believing that Peng Shuai actually wrote the email we received or believes what is being attributed to her."[35]
>
> —Steve Simon, chairman of the Women's Tennis Association

Tennis great Shuai Peng plays at the Australian Open on January 21, 2020. She disappeared in 2021 after making a politically sensitive post on Weibo, the Chinese equivalent of Twitter.

As pressure mounted on China to provide more information, the Peng mystery deepened. The editor of a CCP-run newspaper, the *Global Times*, published several photos of Peng on Twitter. She was holding a cat while surrounded by stuffed animals. There were no dates or time stamps that would indicate when the pictures were taken. The message with the images, written by the editor, said that Peng was resting at home and did not wish to be disturbed.

Observers might see China's handling of the Peng situation as clumsy and heavy-handed, but it shows how government officials try to influence public opinion by manipulating social media. And the Peng incident is not unusual; the CCP often uses social media to spread propaganda. A 2021 study by British disinformation research institute the Centre for Information Resilience (CIR) found a network with thousands of fake social media profiles created by the CCP. These accounts were used to spread distorted pro-China narratives that were critical of the United States and other Western governments. The social media accounts,

Creating Fake People

Government authorities in China have created an extensive network of phony user accounts on social media to spread misinformation and disinformation. Many of the fake profiles use what are called deepfake photos. The realistic-looking people that do not exist are generated by an AI system called StyleGAN. Authorities use this method because AI-generated photos are difficult to trace using reverse image searches. However, British disinformation research institute the Centre for Information Resilience found ways to identify fake profile photos in suspicious accounts.

The AI-generated photos always put the eyes in the same location—within the top one-third of the picture. When the fake photos are put together in a row, a straight line can be drawn through all the eyes. Close examination of the photos also reveal teeth that sometimes appear at odd angles and ears, hair, and other features that appear fuzzy or blurred. Although these odd traits can be detected by experts, photos viewed individually on Twitter, Facebook, and Instagram can easily fool average users.

complete with fake AI-generated profile pictures, were found on Twitter, Facebook, Instagram, and YouTube. According to CIR's executive director, Ross Burley, "The network targets significant subjects such as US gun laws, COVID-19 . . . and racial discrimination in an apparent bid to inflame tensions, [and it attempts to] deny remarks critical of China."[36]

In 2020 Twitter removed more than 23,000 fake CCP accounts that linked to another 150,000 users who spread disinformation. However, these efforts by Twitter and other social media platforms have not slowed the flood of Chinese propaganda.

Political Manipulation

China is an authoritarian dictatorship that might be expected to spread propaganda on social media. But India, often referred to as the world's largest democracy, is also known to use social media for social control. India is governed by Prime Minister Narendra Modi, a member of the right-wing Hindu-nationalist Bharatiya Janata Party (BJP).

The BJP employed one of the most sophisticated social media operations ever developed. Modi is at the center of the operation. He develops political talking points that then are published on a public Google Doc. The document is filled with government-approved tweets, hashtags, and WhatsApp messages. Links to the document are sent to the BJP's social media team, which includes half a million volunteers. These supporters further amplify the messages by copying them and sending them to their friends and family. British digital investigator Benjamin Strick calls this method "copy pasta," which is a type of spam. "They can manipulate every hashtag to get it within the top 10 trending hashtags in India every single day . . . just through this Google Doc campaign,"[37] he says. Although Twitter and others try to ban copy pasta, the platforms mostly detect the spam when it is promoted by computer-managed accounts (bots). Modi sidesteps this issue by using real people to promote his messages.

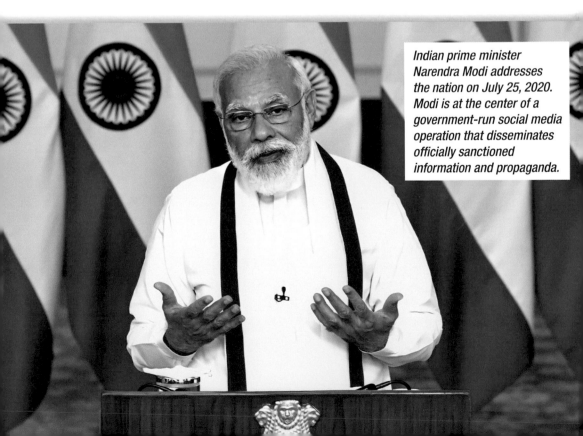

Indian prime minister Narendra Modi addresses the nation on July 25, 2020. Modi is at the center of a government-run social media operation that disseminates officially sanctioned information and propaganda.

Like all political parties and politicians throughout the world, the BJP uses its social media operation to rally voters. But as Mary Louise Kelly, host of NPR's *All Things Considered,* states, "Social media is also where politics can sometimes cross over into disinformation."[38] The BJP crosses that line when it targets Muslims, who are a minority in India.

There has long been tension between Hindus and Muslims in India. In 2020 Hindu nationalist mobs targeted Muslims in vicious riots that broke out in Delhi. The BJP used its social media operation to send out grisly photos of violence supposedly committed by Muslims. The images were fake; the photos were taken in other countries and reflected documented events that had happened in the past. But the phony photos remained on Facebook and other social media platforms even as more than fifty Muslims were senselessly murdered by rampaging rioters.

Facebook is aware of the problems caused by its platform in India, according to internal company documents. In 2019, when an election was approaching, a Facebook employee set up a test account to observe the type of content that was recommended by the platform's algorithms. The employee created a fake profile for a twenty-one-year-old Indian woman. Soon after the account was active, a Muslim suicide bomber killed forty Indian soldiers on the India-Pakistan border. A flood of extremely grisly photos of dead soldiers, beheaded Indian citizens, and other graphic content flooded the Facebook test account. The unnamed Facebook employee who set up the account later wrote, "Following this test user's News Feed, I've seen more images of dead people in the past three weeks than I've seen in my entire life total. . . . The test user's News Feed has become a near constant barrage of polarizing nationalist content, misinformation, and violence and gore."[39]

Facebook had dozens of similar reports about the BJP and party supporters using inflammatory rhetoric against Muslims in India. But there are many obstacles to policing the platform. India has twenty-two officially recognized languages, and Facebook hate speech algorithms only work for five of the most-used tongues. Critics insist that profits are more important than content control. India, which has a population of more than 1.3 billion, is undergoing an economic revolution that is bringing low-cost smartphones to millions of users for the first time. In 2021 Facebook had around 410 million users in India, more than the entire population of the United States. Facebook CEO Zuckerberg has

A Propaganda Battle in India

In February 2019 a Pakistani suicide bomber killed forty Indian soldiers on the India-Pakistan border. As the two countries traded air strikes, a propaganda battle was waged online by Indian government officials hoping to rally voters to support Prime Minister Narendra Modi. Authorities posted a video on social media platforms that supposedly showed Indian fighter jets dropping bombs on Pakistani terrorist camps. The comment underneath the video provided details concerning the attack, including the number of jets, the weight of the bombs, and the exact locations of the camps. The clip, which went viral on Facebook, WhatsApp, and Twitter, was actually a doctored scene taken from a video game. This post was often accompanied by a widely circulated photograph that showed rows of dead bodies wrapped in white shrouds. Although the post explained these were dead Pakistani terrorists, the picture was actually victims who had died during a 2015 heat wave.

The photo and video were the most high-profile examples of propaganda that flooded Indian social media after the suicide bombing. As Trushar Barot, who leads Facebook's antidisinformation efforts in India, tweeted, "I've never seen anything like this before—the scale of fake content circulating on one story."

Quoted in Vindu Goel and Sheera Frenkel, "In India Election, False Posts and Hate Speech Flummox Facebook," *New York Times*, April 1, 2019. www.nytimes.com.

made growing its user numbers in India a company priority and, according to some news sources both inside and outside India, has developed a close relationship with Modi. Although Facebook is aware of hateful, violent content flourishing on its platforms, some observers believe it has been reluctant to censor the BJP, which might interfere with its operations in India.

The New Koo

Facebook only needs to look at Twitter to see what happens to social media companies that anger Modi. In 2021 Indian farmers went on strike to protest agricultural reforms backed by the Modi government. Like millions of others throughout the world, Indian farmers took to Twitter to organize their protests. The Modi government said that farmers were supporting violent demonstrations and demanded that Twitter take down their posts and block some accounts. Twitter refused; executives pointed out that they supported the right to free speech in India and every other nation. Modi threatened to arrest Twitter employees in India. When that failed to solve the dispute, the BJP and its

Koo, a social media app that looks and works like Twitter, is popular in India. It is the go-to platform for Indian officials.

devotees began promoting a little-known Indian social media platform called Koo. The app, which features a bird logo and four-hundred-character posts called Koos, looks and works like Twitter. As dozens of cabinet ministers and high-profile celebrities signed up on Koo, millions of others followed. The company that created the app grew from forty employees to two hundred in less than a year while attracting a $30 million investment from two US venture capital funds that were behind the creation of Facebook in 2004.

> "[Facebook was created] to give people the power to share and make the world more open and connected."[40]
>
> —Mark Zuckerberg, Facebook CEO

Koo has never defied Modi or banned hate speech from his supporters. Although Koo will not likely overtake Twitter's popularity, it has become the go-to platform for officials who want a social media site that has weak content moderation. And Indian politicians are not alone when it comes to promoting pliant social media platforms. In Nigeria, Twitter removed posts by President Muhammadu Buhari for promoting violence in 2021. Buhari banned Twitter and ordered government officials to begin opening accounts on Koo. As the popularity of the app grew in Nigeria, Koo made plans to expand into other African nations as well as into Southeast Asia, eastern Europe, and South America.

When Facebook was created, Zuckerberg wrote in the company's mission statement: "To give people the power to share and make the world more open and connected."[40] It is doubtful that anyone, including Zuckerberg, could have imagined that Facebook or any other social media platform would be used every day by fanatics to foment violence with deceptive photos and bitter hate speech. But with the world divided into clashing political and religious factions, there is nothing to stop politicians and government authorities from manipulating social media to their own ends. This leaves it up to individual social media users to seek facts from reliable sources and ignore emotional appeals from those who would use the power of phony posts to cause harm.

CHAPTER FIVE

Reining In Social Media

In 2021, two seniors at the High School of American Studies in New York City cofounded Teens for Press Freedom (TPF). Charlotte Hampton and Isabel Tribe launched the youth-led organization as a way to challenge social media companies that amplify toxic influencers, fake news, and propaganda. Hampton and Tribe believe that the key to reining in social media is to promote media literacy among their peers.

People with media literacy view social media and other forms of mass communication with a critical eye. They understand how corporations, politicians, and others use media to manipulate and influence the public. Although most young people spend hours a day consuming social media, many lack the media literacy necessary to separate truth from fiction.

Hampton and Tribe created TPF with a view toward future elections. Eight million members of Gen Z will be eligible to vote in 2022, and this group faces divisiveness, political unrest, and environmental disaster on an unprecedented scale. As Hampton and Tribe write, "Social media are riddled with misinformation and disinformation, favoring content designed to provoke. . . . Yet, there is little that helps young people spot

and understand what they're seeing. We're not going to be able to
address global problems unless
we're united on the facts."[41]

Teens for Press Freedom holds
online workshops twice a week
with students from across the
country. Participants examine how
topics such as gun control, climate
change, censorship, and racial jus-
tice are presented on television, in newspapers, and on social
media. And the workshops have changed the way participants
consume media. According to a TPF survey, 90 percent of participants said they have an increased awareness of misinformation and disinformation on social media. One unnamed attendee
said, "I've been more thoroughly checking everything I repost on
Instagram."[42]

Free Speech and Social Media

There is little doubt that consumers of news and information
need to be educated about media bias. And, of course, there is
an app for that. The News Literacy Project, founded by educators, offers a free app that allows users to run down rumors, vet
news for credibility, and expose hoaxes and conspiracies. But
some feel the problem of fake news and propaganda on social
media is so dire that the government needs to take action.

According to a 2021 CNN poll, 53 percent of Americans say
Congress should pass laws that would increase regulation of
Facebook. But the United States is not like China, where government officials can block social media posts and take down
accounts they do not like. The First Amendment of the Consti-
tution guarantees freedom of the press and free speech for all.
This means politicians cannot tell news organizations or private
citizens what they can or cannot say. But after Frances Haugen released Facebook's internal company documents in 2021,

Fake news is not our friend.

We're committed to reducing its spread; so we're working with more fact-checkers globally, improving our technology, and giving you background information on the articles in your News Feed.

Find out more: fb.me/fbchangesUK

facebook

Facebook says it is taking a stand against fake news and propaganda, but critics say the company is not doing enough and that government intervention is needed.

Congress began searching for ways to provide some regulation of influential social media platforms.

Though the government cannot regulate speech, Congress can pass laws that govern corporate behavior. For example, broadcast companies such as NBC and CBS are banned from airing obscene programs due to rules enforced by the Federal Communications Commission. But these laws do not apply to the internet. And social media companies have long been allowed to regulate themselves. TikTok, Facebook, Twitter, and others write their own rules that dictate what can and cannot be posted by users.

Protecting Kids

Some in Congress feel that self-regulation has not gone far enough to limit the potential harms, and in 2021 several bills were proposed to impose stricter government regulations on social media platforms. Most are aimed at protecting children and teens.

One bill would ban features such as video autoplay, push alerts, and even "like" buttons for users fifteen and younger. Another proposal would require social media companies to include what is called an eraser button. By clicking the button, users under the age of eighteen could delete all the personal information collected on them by social media platforms. A more severe regulation would prohibit companies from collecting any personal information from kids and teens without their consent.

Social media companies usually oppose any regulations over their business practices, and they spend a lot of money to prevent new laws from being implemented. For example, Facebook has nearly seventy lobbyists in Washington, DC, who work every day to influence politicians to protect the company's interests. In the months after Haugen testified before Congress in 2021, Facebook spent over $5 million on lobbying—more than the entire Washington influence industry combined. And if tough new laws are passed that interfere with Facebook's business practices, the company will spend many more millions on lawyers to fight the regulations in court.

Facebook has a lot to lose; the personal data the company collects on all its users is worth an estimated $1 trillion. And young people, who are sought-after by advertisers, are a target

Go on an Information Diet

Some disinformation is spread online by users who are trying to convince others to share their biased point of view. Not much can be done to regulate this behavior. But many social media users spread misinformation because they are overwhelmed. They are unable to grasp the accurate news and scientific information they see on traditional news sites and other trusted media sources because there is too much to consume.

In 2020 data science professor Kimon Drakopoulos at the University of Southern California conducted research into political polarization online. He found that it tends to increase when people are simply flooded with too much news, something he calls information inundation. Drakopoulos offers steps to control this problem: "A simple tip to combat misinformation is for platforms to not censor content—which can have very adverse effects—and just control the amount of information that a user is exposed to at a time. This can be a limit in the size of the news feed or a random sampling of only a few articles per topic that are presented to users." This would allow social media users to go on an information diet that might lead to a better outcome for everyone.

Quoted in Emily Gersema, "How Americans Can Help Stop Fake News," USC News, December 1, 2020. https://news.usc.edu.

demographic for this data collection. Perhaps this is why the call to protect kids from social media practices is supported by both Republicans and Democrats in Congress. Although the two opposing parties rarely agree on anything, "one thing that unites Democrats and Republicans is 'Won't someone please think of the children,'" says tech lawyer and free speech expert Gautam Hans. "It's very sellable on a bipartisan basis."[43]

Breaking Up Monopolies

While American lawmakers debate proposals to regulate social media platforms, the Federal Trade Commission (FTC) has taken action on another front. The FTC, which enforces consumer protection laws, fined Facebook $5 billion in 2019 for mishandling users' personal information. The company allowed a consulting firm to harvest user data in order to build political profiles on individuals without their consent. In addition to paying the largest fine ever imposed on a company for violating consumer privacy regulations, Facebook agreed to increase oversight of how it handles user data.

"One thing that unites Democrats and Republicans is 'Won't someone please think of the children.'. . . It's very sellable on a bipartisan basis."[43]

—Gautam Hans, free speech expert

The FTC has other powers that can be used to regulate social media companies. The federal agency is also in charge of enforcing laws to prevent companies from becoming monopolies. Companies that are monopolies control an entire market and have little competition. Regulations that prevent monopolies are called antitrust laws. These rules were originally written during the early twentieth century to break up powerful oil companies and railroads that bought up all their competitors. This allowed them to charge higher prices. One of the most famous antitrust cases, in 1911, resulted in Standard Oil Company being broken up into thirty-four separate companies. Massachusetts senator Elizabeth Warren has proposed doing the same thing to Facebook.

During Warren's unsuccessful 2020 presidential campaign, she ran ads—on Facebook—that referred to the company as a monopoly with vast powers over American democracy. Facebook immediately took down the ads. They were eventually restored,

Senator Elizabeth Warren (D-Mass) speaks during a campaign rally in New York City on March 8, 2019. Warren has proposed breaking up many big technology companies, including Facebook.

but Warren's point was proved; Facebook appeared to use its power to censor political speech it did not like.

Warren was not elected president, but her proposal to break up big tech companies gained traction. (Warren also refers to Amazon and Google as monopolies.) In December 2020 the FTC filed an antitrust lawsuit against Facebook stating that the company "has maintained its monopoly position by buying up companies that present competitive threats and by imposing restrictive policies that . . . [hinder] rivals that Facebook does not or cannot acquire."[44]

The FTC lawsuit was celebrated by Facebook critics, but it will not be settled for many years. And experts in antitrust law say the lawsuit is unlikely to succeed. Traditionally, monopolies were broken up because of the financial harm they caused consumers. But Facebook is free to users. Although some of its business practices might be questionable, consumers are not paying higher prices.

Boycotts Get Attention

Government regulators move at a slow pace. But consumers can use their buying power to force social media companies to change. This was seen during the 2020 protests over the police killing of George Floyd. Social justice groups organized a boycott that grabbed Zuckerberg's attention. In July 2020 several civil rights organizations, including the Color of Change, the National Association for the Advancement of Colored People, and the Anti-Defamation League launched the Stop Hate for Profit campaign. In order to protest how Facebook handled hate speech, campaign organizers persuaded more than four hundred major corporations, including Volkswagen, Adidas, and Microsoft, to stop advertising on the platform. Color of Change founder Rashad Robinson said the Stop Hate for Profit campaign was long overdue: "Facebook has

"[We aim] to force Mark Zuckerberg to address the effect that Facebook has had on our society."[45]

—Rashad Robinson, founder of the Color of Change

Stop Hate for Profit

In 2020 the Stop Hate for Profit campaign persuaded corporate advertisers to boycott Facebook until the company removed racism and hate speech from its platform. Although Facebook banned some users, social justice organizers did not feel the company did enough. In 2021 Stop Hate for Profit called on Facebook to take further steps, including the following:

- Find and remove public and private groups focused on white supremacy, militia, antisemitism, violent conspiracies, vaccine misinformation, and climate denialism.
- Stop recommending or otherwise amplifying groups or content from groups associated with hate, misinformation or conspiracies to users.
- Create an internal mechanism to automatically flag hateful content in private groups for human review. Private groups are not small gatherings of friends—but can be hundreds of thousands of people large, which many hateful groups are.
- Create expert teams to review submissions of identity-based hate and harassment. Forty two percent of daily users of Facebook have experienced harassment on the platform, and much of this harassment is based on the individual's identity. . . .
- Enable individuals facing severe hate and harassment to connect with a live Facebook employee. In no other sector does a company not have a way for victims of their product to seek help.

Stop Hate for Profit, "Recommended Next Steps," 2021. www.stophateforprofit.org.

given [advertisers] no other option because of their failure, time and time again, to address the very real and the very visible problems on their platform. . . . [We aim] to force Mark Zuckerberg to address the effect that Facebook has had on our society."[45]

Facebook and Instagram earned around $70 billion from advertisers in 2019. Stop Hate for Profit posed a threat to this massive revenue stream. Zuckerberg quickly agreed to meet with the campaign's organizers and work with them to reduce hate speech. Zuckerberg also spoke to advertisers during a video meeting in which he outlined policies to ensure their ads would not appear next to hate speech, misinformation, or conspiracy theories. After the meeting, Nick Clegg, Facebook's vice president of global affairs and communications, praised the campaign but did not promise to end all offensive content. "We understand people quite rightly want to put pressure on Facebook to do more," he said. "That's why we'll continue to redouble our efforts, because we have a zero-tolerance approach to hate speech. Unfortunately, zero tolerance doesn't mean zero occurrence."[46]

Demand Change

It might seem impossible to stop the spread of hate on social media when billions of people post an endless stream of content every day. But Clegg's point about putting pressure on Facebook rings true. Government regulations might fail, but corporations will usually pay attention when their profits are at risk. And Facebook executives are aware that their revenues are being threatened. Although the social media giant might seem invincible, some analysts believe Facebook might be facing long-term financial troubles. With the rise of TikTok, the company has become irrelevant to its most important demographic: culture-creating, trendsetting teenagers. Many in this demographic feel Facebook is for their parents.

Facebook might someday go the way of defunct social media sites such as Friendster, but others will rise in its place. And their business practices will likely be widely scrutinized. However, most Americans do not want government bureaucrats deciding who gets to express an opinion on TikTok or Twitter, no matter how ridiculous, so regulation will remain a subject of debate.

In addition, the debate over the power of social media will continue to play out—on social media and elsewhere. Whereas some measures to rein in tech companies might pass legal muster, others will be rejected. In the meantime, it is up to consumers to follow the example set by Teens for Press Freedom. Social media users need to be able to spot fake news and learn to protect their privacy online while demanding that platforms improve. This leaves it up to users to make social media a positive rather than negative experience in their lives.

SOURCE NOTES

Introduction: Motivating the Masses

1. Quoted in Catherine O'Donnell, "New Study Quantifies Use of Social Media in Arab Spring," UW News, University of Washington, September 12, 2011. www.washington.edu.
2. Quoted in Victor Barreiro Jr., "Social Media Helped Radicalize Americans, Fuel January 6 Insurrection—Roger McNamee," Rappler, January 23, 2021. www.rappler.com.
3. Quoted in Jamey Tucker, "What the Tech? How Facebook Makes You Angry," WRCB, October 6, 2021. www.wrcbtv.com.
4. Heather Cox Richardson, *Letters from an American*, Substack newsletter, October 23, 2021. https://heathercoxrichardson.substack.com.
5. Quoted in Katie Canales, "'The Most Powerful Person Who's Ever Walked the Face of the Earth': How Mark Zuckerberg's Stranglehold on Facebook Could Put the Company at Risk," Business Insider, October 13, 2021. www.businessinsider.com.

Chapter One: Raising Awareness

6. Quoted in Jamil Smith, "How the Movement That's Changing America Was Built and Where It Goes Next," *Rolling Stone,* June 16, 2020. www.rollingstone.com.
7. Quoted in Eyder Peralta, "Philando Castile's Girlfriend Speaks Out: 'I Need Justice, I Need Peace," *The Two-Way* (blog), NPR, July 7, 2016. www.npr.org.
8. Quoted in Cydney Henderson, "'John Lewis: Good Trouble': 5 Lessons from the Documentary That Still Apply Today," *USA Today,* July 18, 2020. www.usatoday.com.
9. Quoted in The Federal, "Society Has Passed Tipping Point: Greta Thunberg on Anti-racism Protests," June 20, 2020. https://thefederal.com.
10. Quoted in Jamie Margolin, *Youth to Power: Your Voice and How to Use It.* New York: Hachette, 2020, p. 3.
11. Quoted in Carline Harrap, "Greta Thunberg's Dad: How Fighting for the Climate Changed My Daughter," The Local, December 19, 2019. www.thelocal.se.
12. Quoted in Nadine Zylberberg, "Teens Around the World Are Skipping School to Strike for Climate Action," Medium, July 25, 2019. https://medium.com.
13. Quoted in Deutsche Welle, "Has COVID Changed Fridays for Future?," March 19, 2021. www.dw.com.

14. Alec Tyson, Brian Kennedy, and Cary Funk, "Gen Z, Millennials Stand Out for Climate Change Activism, Social Media Engagement with Issue," Pew Research Center, May 26, 2021. www.pewresearch.org.

Chapter Two: The Influence of Influencers

15. Quoted in Meg Zukin, "Why TikTok Stars Will Survive No Matter What," *Variety*, August 4, 2020. https://variety.com.
16. Quoted in Zukin, "Why TikTok Stars Will Survive No Matter What."
17. Quoted in Natalie Robehmed, "At 21, Kylie Jenner Becomes the Youngest Self-Made Billionaire Ever," *Forbes,* March 5, 2019. www.forbes.com.
18. Quoted in Dan Milmo and Kari Paul, "Facebook Disputes Its Own Research Showing Harmful Effects of Instagram on Teens' Mental Health," *The Guardian,* September 30, 2021. www.theguardian.com.
19. Quoted in Derek Thompson, "Social Media Is Attention Alcohol," *The Atlantic,* September 17, 2021. www.theatlantic.com.
20. Laurence Steinberg, "Does Instagram Harm Girls? No One Actually Knows," *New York Times,* October 10, 2021. www.nytimes.com.
21. Quoted in Kari Paul, "'It Spreads Like a Disease': How Pro-Eating-Disorder Videos Reach Teens on TikTok," *The Guardian,* October 16, 2017. www.theguardian.com.
22. Quoted in Paul, "'It Spreads Like a Disease.'"
23. Quoted in Paul, "'It Spreads Like a Disease.'"
24. Quoted in Kelly Burch, "How to Break Social Media Addiction, or Spend Less Time Online," Insider, May 14, 2020. www.insider.com.

Chapter Three: Spreading Fear, Mistrust, and Lies

25. Quoted in Brandy Zadrozny, "'Carol's Journey': What Facebook Knew About How It Radicalized Users," NBC News, October 22, 2021. www.nbcnews.com.
26. Quoted in Travis M. Andrews, "She Fell Into QAnon and Went Viral for Destroying a Target Mask Display. Now She's Rebuilding Her Life," *Washington Post,* November 11, 2020. www.washingtonpost.com.
27. Quoted in Kevin Roose, "The Making of a YouTube Radical," *New York Times,* June 8, 2019. www.nytimes.com.
28. Quoted in Jeremy B. Merrill and Will Oremus, "Five Points for Anger, One for a 'Like': How Facebook's Formula Fostered Rage and Misinformation," *Washington Post,* October 26, 2021. www.washingtonpost.com.
29. Quoted in Craig Timberg, Elizabeth Dwoskin, and Reed Albergotti, "Inside Facebook, Jan. 6 Violence Fueled Anger, Regret over Missed Warning Signs," *Washington Post,* October 22, 2021. www.washingtonpost.com.
30. Quoted in Shannon Bond and Bobby Allyn, "How the 'Stop the Steal' Movement Outwitted Facebook Ahead of the Jan. 6 Insurrection," NPR, October 22, 2021. www.npr.org.
31. Quoted in Alexandra S. Levine, "Inside Facebook's Struggle to Contain Insurrectionists' Posts," Politico, October 25, 2021. www.politico.com.

32. Quoted in Elizabeth Dwoskin and Cat Zakrewski, "Facebook's Oversight Board Upholds Ban on Trump. At Least for Now," *Washington Post,* May 5, 2021. www.washingtonpost.com.
33. Quoted in Alex Heath, "Mark Zuckerberg Breaks Silence to Say the Facebook Whistleblower's Claims 'Don't Make Any Sense,'" *The Verge* (blog), October 5, 2021. www.theverge.com.

Chapter Four: Social Media or Social Control?

34. Quoted in Wajih AlBaroudi, "Peng Shuai Situation Explained: WTA Suspends All Tournaments in China amid Censorship of Former World No. 1," CBS Sports, December 1, 2021. www.cbssports.com.
35. Quoted in Helen Regan, Nectar Gan, and Rhea Mogul, "Doubt Cast on Alleged Email from Tennis Star Peng Shuai amid Worries over Her Whereabouts," CNN Sports, November 18, 2021. www.cnn.com.
36. Ross Burley, "Revealed: Coordinated Attempt to Push Pro-China, Anti-Western Narratives on Social Media," Centre for Information Resilience, August 4, 2021. http://info-res.org.
37. Quoted in Lauren Frayer, "How India Is Confronting Disinformation on Social Media Ahead of Elections," *All Things Considered,* NPR, April 22, 2021. www.npr.org.
38. Quoted in Frayer, "How India Is Confronting Disinformation on Social Media Ahead of Elections."
39. Quoted in Sheera Frenkel and Davey Alba, "In India, Facebook Grapples with an Amplified Version of Its Problems," *New York Times,* October 23, 2021. www.nytimes.com.
40. Quoted in Michael J. Coren, "Facebook's Global Expansion No Longer Has Its Mission Statement Standing in the Way," Quartz, June 22, 2017. https://qz.com.

Chapter Five: Reining In Social Media

41. Charlotte Hampton and Isabel Tribe, "Gen Z Needs to Get Our Act Together Before We Vote in Next Year's Midterms," *Los Angeles Times,* October 25, 2021. www.latimes.com.
42. Quoted in Hampton and Tribe, "Gen Z Needs to Get Our Act Together Before We Vote in Next Year's Midterms."
43. Quoted in Marcy Gordon, "After Facebook Papers, How Will Congress Regulate Social Media?," *Christian Science Monitor,* November 1, 2021. www.csmonitor.com.
44. Quoted in Matthew Rozsa, "'Wrath of Mark': Antitrust Lawsuits Against Facebook Accuse Zuckerberg of Stifling Competition," Salon, December 10, 2020. www.salon.com.
45. Quoted in Shannon Bond, "Over 400 Advertisers Hit Pause on Facebook, Threatening $70 Billion Juggernaut," NPR, July 1, 2020. www.npr.org.
46. Quoted in Bond, "Over 400 Advertisers Hit Pause on Facebook, Threatening $70 Billion Juggernaut."

ORGANIZTIONS AND WEBSITES

Black Lives Matter (BLM)

https://blacklivesmatter.com

The BLM website features news about the movement and information about the latest protests and other actions. Users can download tool kits with learning materials about conflict resolution, race relations, and COVID-19.

Centre for Information Resilience (CIR)

www.info-res.org

This British organization exposes and counters individuals and groups that use social media to spread disinformation. CIR works with a global network to counter these threats to democracy.

Girls Leading Others Wisely (GLOW)

www.glowprogram.com

GLOW was founded to help girls develop skills to enhance their self-confidence and resist peer pressure on social media. The website features over 12 hours of curriculum meant to empower girls by increasing their strengths and abilities.

News Literacy Project

https://newslit.org

The News Literacy Project is a nonpartisan organization founded by educators to teach young people ways to become smart, active consumers of news and information. The site offers an online learning platform, a free app, podcasts, and shareable tips, tools, and quizzes aimed at increasing media literacy.

Teens for Press Freedom (TPF)

www.teensforpressfreedom.org

This youth-led organization was founded to promote media literacy among high school students. The group hosts twice-weekly online workshops about news consumption and misinformation and disinformation on social media.

FOR FURTHER RESEARCH

Books

Goali Saedi Bocci, *The Social Media Workbook for Teens: Skills to Help You Balance Screen Time, Manage Stress, and Take Charge of Your Life*. Oakland, CA: Instant Help, 2019.

Lori Getz and Mitch Prinstein, *Like Ability: The Truth About Popularity*. Washington, DC: Magination, 2022.

Marcia S. Gresko, *How Should Extremist Content Be Regulated on Social Media?* San Diego: ReferencePoint, 2020.

Jamie Margolin, *Youth to Power: Your Voice and How to Use It*. New York: Hachette, 2020.

Bradley Steffens, *The Dark Side of Social Media*. San Diego: Reference-Point, 2022.

Internet Sources

Victor Barreiro Jr., "Social Media Helped Radicalize Americans, Fuel January 6 Insurrection—Roger McNamee," Rappler, January 23, 2021. www.rappler.com.

Sheera Frenkel and Davey Alba, "In India, Facebook Grapples with an Amplified Version of Its Problems," *New York Times,* October 23, 2021. www.nytimes.com.

Charlotte Hampton and Isabel Tribe, "Gen Z Needs to Get Our Act Together Before We Vote in Next Year's Midterms," *Los Angeles Times,* October 25, 2021. www.latimes.com.

Heather Cox Richardson, *Letters from an American*, Substack newsletter, October 23, 2021. https://heathercoxrichardson.substack.com.

Jamil Smith, "How the Movement That's Changing America Was Built and Where It Goes Next," *Rolling Stone,* June 16, 2020. www.rollingstone.com.

Derek Thompson, "Social Media Is Attention Alcohol," *The Atlantic,* September 17, 2021. www.theatlantic.com.

INDEX